50 stitches for Afghans™

Square 1

Multiple of 3 + 6

PATTERN NOTE
Chain-3 at beginning of row counts as first double crochet unless otherwise stated.

SPECIAL STITCH
V-stitch (V-st): (Dc, ch 1, dc) in indicated place.

INSTRUCTIONS
SQUARE
Row 1 (RS): 3 dc in 4th ch from hook (*first 3 chs count as first dc*), [sk next 2 chs, 3 dc in next ch] across to last 2 chs, sk next ch, dc in last ch, turn.

Row 2: **Ch 3** (*see Pattern Note*), **V-st** (*see Special Stitch*) in center st of each 3-dc group across to last st, dc in 3rd ch of beg sk 3 chs, turn.

Row 3: Ch 3, 3 dc in ch sp of each V-st across to last st, dc in 3rd ch of beg ch-3, turn.

Row 4: Ch 3, V-st in center st of each 3-dc group across to last st, dc in 3rd ch of beg ch-3, turn.

Rep rows 3 and 4 for pattern, ending last rep with row 3. ■

Square 2

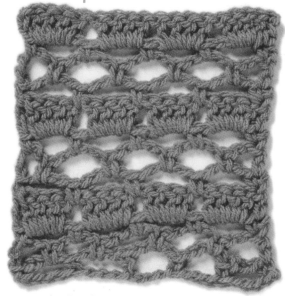

Multiple of 4 + 6

PATTERN NOTE
Chain-3 at beginning of row counts as first double crochet unless otherwise stated.

INSTRUCTIONS
SQUARE
Row 1 (RS): Sc in 2nd ch from hook, [ch 4, sk next 3 chs, sc in next st] across, turn.

Row 2: Ch 5 *(counts as first dc and ch-2 sp)*, sc in next ch sp, [ch 4, sc in next ch sp] across, ch 2, dc in last st, turn.

Row 3: Ch 1, sc in first st, [ch 3, sc in next ch-4 sp] across to last ch-2 sp, ch 3, sc in 3rd ch of beg ch-5, turn.

Row 4: Ch 3 *(see Pattern Note)*, 4 dc in each ch-3 sp across to last st, dc in last st, turn.

Row 5: Ch 1, sc in first st, working in sps between 4-dc groups, [ch 4, sc in next sp between 4-dc groups] across to last 4-dc group, ch 4, sc in 3rd ch of beg ch-3, turn.

Row 6: Ch 5 *(counts as first dc and ch-2 sp)*, sc in first ch sp, [ch 4, sc in next ch sp] across, ch 2, dc in last st, turn.

Row 7: Ch 1, sc in first st, [ch 3, sc in next ch-4 sp] across to last ch-2 sp, ch 3, sc in 3rd ch of beg ch-5, turn.

Row 8: Ch 3, 4 dc in each ch-3 sp across to last st, dc in last st, turn.

Rep rows 5–8 for pattern. ∎

Square 3

Multiple of 6 + 8

SPECIAL STITCH
Front post triple decrease (fp triple dec): Yo, insert hook in next ch-1 sp, yo, pull lp through, yo, pull through 2 lps on hook, yo, insert hook from front to back around post of next st, yo, pull lp through, yo, pull through 2 lps on hook, yo, insert hook in next ch-1 sp, yo, pull lp through, yo, pull through 2 lps on hook, yo, pull through all 4 lps on hook.

INSTRUCTIONS
SQUARE
Row 1 (RS): Sc in 2nd ch from hook, [ch 3, sk next ch, **dc dec** *(see Stitch Guide)* in next 3 chs, ch 3, sk next ch, sc in next ch] across, turn.

Row 2: Ch 5 *(counts as first dc and ch-2 sp)*, sc in next ch sp, ch 1, sc in next ch sp, ch 1, dc in next sc, *[ch 1, sc in next ch sp] twice, ch 1, dc in next sc, rep from * across, turn.

Row 3: Ch 2 *(not used or counted as a st)*, dc in next ch-1 sp, ch 4, sc in next ch-1 sp, ch 4, [**fp triple dec** *(see Special Stitch)*, ch 4, sc in next ch-1 sp, ch 4] across to last ch sp, dc dec in last ch sp and in 3rd ch of beg ch-5 dc, turn.

Row 4: Ch 1, sc in first st, sc in next ch-4 sp, ch 1, dc in next sc, ch 1, sc in next ch-4 sp, [ch 1, sc in next ch-4 sp, ch 1, dc in next sc, ch 1, sc in next ch-4 sp] across to last st, sc in last st, turn.

Row 5: Ch 1, sc in first st, ch 4, fp triple dec, ch 4, [sc in next ch-1 sp, ch 4, fp triple dec, ch 4] across to last st, sc in last st, turn.

Rep rows 2–5 for pattern. ■

Square 4

Multiple of 12 + 16

PATTERN NOTE
Chain-3 at beginning of row counts as first double crochet unless otherwise stated.

INSTRUCTIONS
SQUARE
Row 1 (RS): 3 dc in 4th ch from hook *(first 3 chs count as first dc)*, sk next 5 chs, 4 dc in next ch,

ch 3, sk next 2 chs, sc in next ch, ch 3, sk next 2 chs, [4 dc in next ch, sk next 5 chs, 4 dc in next ch, ch 3, sk next 2 chs, sc in next ch, ch 3, sk next 2 chs] across to last ch, dc in last ch, turn.

Row 2: **Ch 3** *(see Pattern Note)*, 3 dc in same st, 4 dc in first st of next 4-dc group, ch 3, sc in sp between this 4-dc group and next 4-dc group, ch 3, [4 dc in 4th st of next 4-dc group, 4 dc in first st of next 4th dc group, ch 3, sc in sp between this 4-dc group and next 4-dc group, ch 3] across, dc in 3rd ch of beg 3 sk chs, turn.

Row 3: Ch 3, 3 dc in same st, 4 dc in first st of next 4-dc group, ch 3, sc in sp between this 4-dc group and next 4-dc group, ch 3, [4 dc in 4th st of next 4-dc group, 4 dc in first st of next 4th dc group, ch 3, sc in sp between this 4-dc group and next 4-dc group, ch 3] across, dc in 3rd ch of beg ch-3, turn.

Rep row 3 for pattern. ■

Square 5

Multiple of 14 + 17

PATTERN NOTES
Chain-3 at beginning of row counts as first double crochet unless otherwise stated.

Chain-5 at beginning of row counts as first double crochet and chain-2 space unless otherwise stated.

SPECIAL STITCHES

V-stitch (V-st): (Dc, ch 1, dc) in indicated place.

Shell: (3 dc, ch 1, 3 dc) in indicated place.

INSTRUCTIONS
SQUARE

Row 1 (RS): Dc in 4th ch from hook *(first 3 chs count as first dc)* and in each ch across, turn.

Row 2: Ch 5 *(see Pattern Notes)*, sk next 3 sts, **V-st** *(see Special Stitches)* in next st, ch 2, sk next 3 sts, dc in each of next 7 sts, [ch 2, sk next 3 sts, V-st in next st, ch 2, sk next 3 sts, dc in each of next 7 sts] across to last st, dc in 3rd ch of beg 3 sk chs, turn.

Row 3: **Ch 3** *(see Pattern Notes)*, sk first st, [dc in each of next 7 sts, sk next ch-2 sp, **shell** *(see Special Stitches)* in ch sp of next V-st, sk next ch-2 sp] across to last st, dc in 3rd ch of beg ch-5, turn.

Row 4: Ch 5, V-st in ch sp of next shell, ch 2, sk next 3 sts of same shell, dc in each of next 7 sts, [ch 2, V-st in ch sp of next shell, ch 2, sk next 3 sts of same shell, dc in each of next 7 sts] across to last st, dc in 3rd ch of beg ch-3, turn.

Row 5: Ch 3, dc in each st across to last st with 2 dc in each ch-2 sp and dc in each ch-1 sp, 2 dc in last ch sp and dc in 3rd ch of beg ch-5, turn.

Row 6: Ch 3, sk first st, [dc in each of next 7 sts, ch 2, sk next 3 sts, V-st in next st, ch 2, sk next 3 sts] across to last st, dc in 3rd ch of beg ch-3, turn.

Row 7: Ch 3, [sk next ch sp, shell in ch sp of next V-st, sk next ch sp, dc in each of next 7 sts] across to last st, dc in 3rd ch of beg ch-3. turn.

Row 8: Ch 3, [dc in each of next 7 sts, ch 2, V-st in ch sp of next shell, ch 2, sk next 3 sts of same shell] across to last st, dc in 3rd ch of beg ch-3, turn.

Row 9: Ch 3, dc in each st across to last st with 2 dc in each ch-2 sp and dc in each ch-1 sp, dc in 3rd ch of beg ch-3, turn.

Row 10: Ch 5, sk next 3 sts, V-st in next st, ch 2, sk next 3 sts, dc in each of next 7 sts, [ch 2,

sk next 3 sts, V-st in next st, ch 2, sk next 3 sts, dc in each of next 7 sts] across to last st, dc in 3rd ch of beg ch-3, turn.

Rep rows 3–10 for pattern, ending last rep at row 9. ∎

Square 6

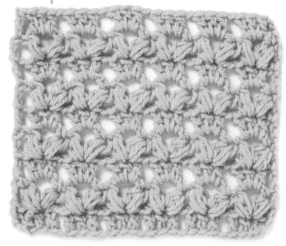

Multiple of 4 + 7

PATTERN NOTE

Chain-3 at beginning of row counts as first double crochet unless otherwise stated.

SPECIAL STITCH

Puff stitch (puff st): Yo, insert hook in indicated st, yo, pull lp through, [yo, insert hook in same st, yo, pull lp through] twice, yo, pull through all 7 lps on hook.

INSTRUCTIONS
SQUARE

Row 1 (RS): Dc in 4th ch from hook *(first 3 chs count as first dc)*, dc in each of next 2 chs, [ch 1, sk next ch, dc in each of next 3 chs] across to last ch, dc in last ch, turn.

Row 2: **Ch 3** *(see Pattern Note)*, sk next 2 sts, **puff st** *(see Special Stitch)* in next st, ch 4, puff st in same st, (puff st, ch 4, puff st) in center st of each 3-dc group across to last st, dc in 3rd ch of beg 3 sk chs, turn.

Row 3: Ch 3, (3 dc, ch 1) in each ch-4 sp across to last ch-4 sp, 3 dc in last ch-4 sp, dc in 3rd ch of beg ch-3, turn.

Row 4: Ch 3, sk next 2 sts, puff st in next st, ch 4, puff st in same st, (puff st, ch 4, puff st) in center st of each 3-dc group across to last st, dc in 3rd ch of beg ch-3, turn.

Rep rows 3 and 4 for pattern, ending last rep at row 3. ■

Square 7

Multiple of 8 + 2

PATTERN NOTE
Chain-3 at beginning of row counts as first double crochet unless otherwise stated.

INSTRUCTIONS
SQUARE
Row 1 (RS): Sc in 2nd ch from hook, [sk next 3 chs, 9 dc in next ch, sk next 3 chs, sc in next ch] across, turn.

Row 2: Ch 3 (see Pattern Note), sk first sc, *sk next dc, **dc dec** (see Stitch Guide) in next 3 sts, ch 3, sc in next st, ch 3, dc dec in next 3 sts, ch 1, sk next dc**, sk next sc, rep from * across to last st, ending last rep at **, dc in last st, turn.

Row 3: Ch 1, sc in first st, 9 dc in next sc, [sc in next ch-1 sp, 9 dc in next sc] across to last st, sc in 3rd ch of beg ch-3, turn.

Rep rows 2 and 3 for pattern. ■

Square 8

Multiple of 6 + 6

PATTERN NOTE
Chain-3 at beginning of row counts as first double crochet unless otherwise stated.

SPECIAL STITCHES
Shell: (Dc, {ch 1, dc} 4 times) in indicated st.

Picot: Ch 3, sl st in 3rd ch from hook.

INSTRUCTIONS
SQUARE
Row 1: Sc in 2nd ch from hook, ch 3, sk next 3 chs, sc in next ch, [ch 2, sk next ch, sc in next ch, ch 3, sk next 3 chs, sc in next ch] across, turn.

Row 2 (RS): Ch 3 (see Pattern Note), **shell** (see Special Stitches) in next ch-3 sp, [**picot** (see Special Stitches), shell in next ch-3 sp] across to last st, dc in last st, turn.

Row 3: Ch 1, sc in first st, ch 1, sc in 2nd ch-1 sp of next shell, ch 1, sc in next ch-1 sp of same shell, [ch 3, sc in 2nd ch sp of next shell, ch 1, sc in next ch-1 sp of same shell] across to last st, ch 1, sc in 3rd ch of beg ch-3, turn.

Row 4: Ch 4 (*counts as first dc and ch-1 sp*), (dc, ch 1, dc) in same st, [picot, shell in next ch-3 sp] across, picot, (dc, {ch 1, dc} twice) in last st, turn.

Row 5: Ch 1, sc in first st and in first ch-1 sp, ch 3, [sc in 2nd ch-1 sp of next shell, ch 2, sc in next ch-1 sp of same shell, ch 3] across to last ch sp and st, sc in last ch sp and in 3rd ch of beg ch-4, turn.

Row 6: Ch 3, shell in next ch-3 sp, [picot, shell in next ch-3 sp] across to last st, dc in last st, turn.

Rep rows 3–6 for pattern. ■

Square 9

Multiple of 4 + 4

SPECIAL STITCH
Puff stitch (puff st): Yo, insert hook in indicated st, yo, pull lp through, [yo, insert hook in same st, yo, pull lp through] twice, yo, pull through all 7 lps on hook.

INSTRUCTIONS
SQUARE
Row 1 (RS): Sc in 2nd ch from hook and in each ch across, turn.

Row 2: Ch 1, sc in each of first 3 sts, [**puff st** (*see Special Stitch*) in next st, sc in each of next 3 sts] across, turn.

Row 3: Ch 1, sc in each st across, turn.

Row 4: Ch 1, sc in first st, [puff st in next st, sc in each of next 3 sts] across to last 2 sts, puff st in next st, sc in last st, turn.

Row 5: Ch 1, sc in each st across, turn.

Rep rows 2–5 for pattern. ■

Square 10

Multiple of 8 + 9

PATTERN NOTE
Chain-3 at beginning of row counts as first double crochet unless otherwise stated.

SPECIAL STITCH
Popcorn (pc): 5 dc in indicated place, drop lp from hook, insert hook from back to front through first of 5-dc group, pull dropped lp through.

INSTRUCTIONS
SQUARE
Row 1 (RS): Dc in 4th ch from hook (*first 3 chs count as first dc*), dc in each of next 5 sts, [ch 1, sk next ch, dc in each of next 7 chs] across, turn.

Row 2: **Ch 3** (*see Pattern Note*), sk first st, dc in each of next 2 sts, **pc** (*see Special Stitch*) in next st, dc in each of next 3 sts, *ch 1, sk next ch sp, dc in each of next 3 sts, pc in next st**, dc in each of next 3 sts, rep from * across, ending last rep at **, dc in each of next 2 sts, dc in 3rd ch of beg 3 sk chs, turn.

Row 3: Ch 3, sk first st, dc in each of next 6 sts or ch sps, *ch 1, sk next ch sp**, dc in each of next 7 sts or ch sps, rep from * across, ending last rep at **, dc in each of next 6 sts or ch sps, dc in 3rd ch of beg ch-3, turn.

Row 4: Ch 4 *(counts as first dc and ch-1 sp)*, sk next st, dc in next st, *ch 1, sk next st or ch sp**, dc in next st, rep from * across, ending last rep at **, dc in 3rd ch of beg ch-3, turn.

Row 5: Ch 3, sk first st, dc in each of next 6 sts or ch sps, *ch 1, sk next ch sp**, dc in each of next 7 sts or ch sps, rep from * across, ending last rep at **, dc in each of next 6 chs, dc in 3rd ch of beg ch-4, turn.

Row 6: Ch 3, sk first st, dc in each of next 2 sts, pc in next st, dc in each of next 3 sts, *ch 1, sk next ch sp, dc in each of next 3 sts, pc in next st**, dc in each of next 3 sts, rep from * across, ending last rep at **, dc in each of next 2 sts, sc in 3rd ch of beg ch-3, turn.

Row 7: Ch 3, dc in each of next 6 sts, *ch 1, sk next ch sp**, dc in each of next 7 sts or ch sps, rep from * across, ending last rep at **, dc in each of next 6 sts, dc in 3rd ch of beg ch-3, turn.

Rep rows 4–7 for pattern. ■

Square 11

Multiple of 11 + 5

PATTERN NOTE
Chain-3 at beginning of row counts as first double crochet unless otherwise stated.

INSTRUCTIONS
SQUARE
Row 1: Dc in 4th ch from hook *(first 3 chs count as first dc)* and in each ch across, turn.

Row 2 (RS): **Ch 3** *(see Pattern Note)*, sk first st, dc in each of next 2 sts, *ch 3, sk next 2 sts, tr in each of next 4 sts, ch 3, sk next 2 sts**, dc in each of next 3 sts, rep from * across, ending last rep at **, dc in each of next 2 sts, dc in 3rd ch of beg 3 sk chs, turn.

Rows 3–5: Ch 3, sk first st, dc in each of next 2 sts, *ch 3, sk next ch sp, sc in each of next 4 sts, ch 3, sk next ch sp**, dc in each of next 3 sts, rep from * across, ending last rep at **, dc in each of next 2 sts, dc in 3rd ch of beg ch-3, turn.

Row 6: Ch 3, sk first st, dc in each of next 2 sts, *ch 3, sk next ch sp, tr in each of next 4 sts, ch 3, sk next ch sp**, dc in each of next 3 sts, rep from * across, ending last rep at **, dc in each of next 2 sts, dc in 3rd ch of beg ch-3, turn.

Row 7: Ch 3, sk first st, work dc in each st with 2 dc in each ch-3 sp across to last st, dc in 3rd ch of beg ch-3, turn.

Row 8: Ch 3, sk first st, dc in each of next 2 sts, *ch 3, sk next 2 sts, tr in each of next 4 sts, ch 3, sk next 2 sts**, dc in each of next 3 sts, rep from * across, ending last rep at **, dc in each of last 2 sts, dc in 3rd ch of beg ch-3, turn.

Rep rows 3–8 for pattern, ending last rep at row 7. ■

Square 12

Multiple of 6 + 5

PATTERN NOTE
Chain-3 at beginning of row counts as first double crochet unless otherwise stated.

SPECIAL STITCH
Back post double crochet decrease (bpdc dec):
Yo, insert hook from back to front around post of next post st, yo, pull lp through, yo, pull through 2 lps on hook, yo, insert hook from back to front around post of next post st, yo, pull lp through, yo, pull through 2 lps on hook, yo, pull through all 3 lps on hook.

INSTRUCTIONS
SQUARE
Row 1 (RS): Dc in 4th ch from hook (*first 3 chs count as first dc*) and in each ch across, turn

Row 2: Ch 3 (*see Pattern Note*), sk first st, dc in each of next 2 sts, *sk next st, **bpdc** (*see Stitch Guide*) around next st, dc in same st, bpdc around same st, sk next st**, dc in each of next 3 sts, rep from * across, ending last rep at **, dc in each of next 2 sts, dc in 3rd ch of beg sk 3 chs, turn.

Row 3: Ch 3, sk first st, dc in next st, sk next st, **fpdc** (*see Stitch Guide*) around next post st, dc in same st, dc in each of next 2 sts, fpdc around same st as last dc, [sk next st, dc in next st, sk next st, fpdc around next post st, dc in same st, dc in each of next 2 sts, fpdc around same st as last dc] across to last 3 sts, sk next st, dc in next st, dc in 3rd ch of beg ch-3, turn.

Row 4: Ch 3, sk next st, bpdc around next post st, dc in same st, dc in each of next 4 sts, [**bpdc dec** (*see Special Stitch*) around same st as last dc and next post st, dc in same st as last st of dec, dc in each of next 4 sts] across to last 2 sts, bpdc around same st as last st of dec, sk next st, dc in 3rd ch of beg ch-3, turn.

Row 5: Ch 3, dc in each st across to last st, dc in 3rd ch of beg ch-3, turn.

Row 6: Ch 3, sk first st, dc in each of next 2 sts, *sk next st, bpdc around next st, dc in same st, bpdc around same st, sk next st**, dc in each of next 3 sts, rep from * across, ending last rep at **, dc in each of next 2 sts, dc in 3rd ch of beg ch-3, turn.

Rep rows 3–6 for pattern, ending last rep with row 5. ■

Square 13

Multiple of 8 + 11

SPECIAL STITCH

Puff stitch (puff st): Yo, insert hook in indicated st, yo, pull lp through, [yo, insert hook in same st, yo, pull lp through] twice, yo, pull through all 7 lps on hook.

INSTRUCTIONS
SQUARE

Row 1 (RS): **Puff st** (*see Special Stitch*) in 8th ch from hook (*first 7 chs count as first dc, ch-1 sp and sk 3 chs*), ch 3, puff st in same ch, [sk next 3 chs, dc in next ch, ch 1, sk next 3 chs, (puff st, ch 3, puff st) in next ch] across to last 3 chs, ch 1, sk next 2 chs, dc in last ch, turn.

Row 2: Ch 4 (*counts as first dc and ch-1 sp*), sk first st, (puff st, ch 3, puff st) in next ch-3 sp, [dc in next dc, ch 1, (puff st, ch 3, puff st) in next ch 3 sp] across to last st, dc in 3rd ch of beg 7 sk chs, turn.

Row 3: Ch 4, sk first st, (puff st, ch 3, puff st) in next ch-3 sp, [dc in next dc, ch 1, (puff st, ch 3, puff st) in next ch 3 sp] across to last st, dc in 3rd ch of beg ch-4, turn.

Rep row 3 for pattern. ■

Square 14

Multiple of 7 + 9

PATTERN NOTE

Chain-3 at beginning of row counts as first double crochet unless otherwise stated.

SPECIAL STITCHES

V-stitch (V-st): (Dc, ch 1, dc) in indicated place.

Horizontal cluster (horizontal cl): Yo, insert hook around posts of last 3 dc made at same time, yo, pull up long lp, yo, pull through 2 lps on hook, [yo, insert hook around posts of same 3 sts at same time, yo, pull up long lp, yo, pull through 2 lps on hook] twice, yo, pull lp through all 4 lps on hook.

INSTRUCTIONS
SQUARE

Row 1 (RS): Dc in 5th ch from hook (*first 4 chs count as first dc and first sk ch*), dc in each of next 2 chs, **horizontal cl** (*see Special Stitches*), [sk next 2 chs, **V-st** (*see Special Stitches*) in next ch, sk next ch, dc in each of next 3 chs, horizontal cl] across to last 2 chs, sk next ch, dc in last ch, turn

Row 2: **Ch 3** (*see Pattern Note*), sk first st, *dc in next horizontal cl, dc in each of next 3 dc**, V-st in ch sp of next V-st, rep from * across, ending last rep at **, dc in 3rd ch of beg 4 sk chs, turn.

Row 3: Ch 3, sk first st, dc in each of next 3 sts, horizontal cl, sk next st, [V-st in ch sp of next V-st, sk next st of same V-st, dc in each of next 3 sts, horizontal cl, sk next st] across to last st, dc in 3rd ch of beg ch-3, turn.

Row 4: Ch 3, sk first st, *dc in next horizontal cl, dc in each of next 3 dc**, V-st in ch sp of next V-st, rep from * across, ending last rep at **, dc in 3rd ch of beg ch-3, turn.

Rep rows 3 and 4 for pattern, ending last rep with row 3. ■

Square 15

Multiple of 10 + 11

INSTRUCTIONS
SQUARE
Row 1 (RS): Dc in 4th ch from hook (*first 3 chs count as first dc*), sk next ch, (4 dc, ch 2, dc) in next ch, sk next 3 chs, [dc in each of next 5 chs, sk next ch, (4 dc, ch 2, dc) in next ch, sk next 3 chs] across to last 2 chs, dc in each of last 2 chs, turn.

Row 2: Ch 3 (*counts as first dc*), sk first st, dc in next st, (4 dc, ch 2, dc) in next ch-2 sp, sk next 4 sts, [dc in each of next 5 sts, (4 dc, ch 2, dc) in next ch-2 sp, sk next 4 sts] across to last 2 sts, dc next st, dc in 3rd ch of beg 3 sk chs, turn.

Row 3: Ch 3 (*counts as first dc*), sk first st, dc in next st, (4 dc, ch 2, dc) in next ch-2 sp, sk next 4 sts, [dc in each of next 5 sts, (4 dc, ch 2, dc) in next ch-2 sp, sk next 4 sts] across to last 2 sts, dc next st, dc in 3rd ch of beg ch-3, turn.

Rep row 3 for pattern. ■

Square 16

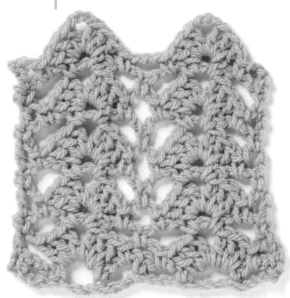

Multiple of 12 + 14

INSTRUCTIONS
SQUARE
Row 1: Sc in 2nd ch from hook, [ch 3, sk next 3 sts, sc in next st] across, turn.

Row 2 (RS): Ch 4 (*counts as first dc and ch-1 sp*), sk first st, sc in next ch sp, (3 dc, ch 3, 3 dc) in next ch sp, sc in next ch sp, *ch 3, sc in next ch sp, (3 dc, ch 3, 3 dc) in next ch sp, sc in next ch sp, rep from * across to last st, ch 1, dc in last st, turn.

Row 3: Ch 1, sc in first st, ch 3, (sc, ch 3, sc) in next ch-3 sp, [ch 3, sc in next ch sp, ch 3, (sc, ch 3, sc) in next ch sp] across, ch 3, sc in 3rd ch of beg ch-4, turn.

Rep rows 2 and 3 for pattern. ■

Square  17

Multiple of 13 + 8

PATTERN NOTES

Chain-4 at beginning of row counts as first double crochet and chain-1 space unless otherwise stated.

Chain-5 at beginning of row counts as first double crochet and chain-2 space unless otherwise stated.

Chain-3 at beginning of row counts as first double crochet unless otherwise stated.

SPECIAL STITCH

V-stitch (V-st): (Dc, ch 1, dc) in indicated place.

INSTRUCTIONS

SQUARE

Row 1: V-st *(see Special Stitch)* in 9th ch from hook *(first 8 chs count as first dc, sk 3 chs and ch-2 sp)*, ch 2, sk next 3 chs, dc in next ch, [ch 2, sk next 3 chs, V-st in next ch, ch 2, sk next 3 chs, dc in next ch] across, turn.

Row 2 (RS): **Ch 5** *(see Pattern Notes)*, 3 dc in ch sp of next V-st, ch 2, dc in next dc, *ch 2, 3 dc in ch sp of next V-st, ch 2**, dc in next dc,

rep from * across, ending last rep at **, dc in 5th ch of beg 8 sk chs, turn.

Row 3: **Ch 4** *(see Pattern Notes)*, 5 dc in center st of next 3-dc group, ch 1, dc in next dc, *ch 1, 5 dc in center st of next 3-dc group, ch 1**, dc in next dc, rep from * across, ending last rep at **, dc in 3rd ch of beg ch-5, turn.

Row 4: Ch 4, 7 dc in center st of next 5-dc group, ch 1, dc in next dc, *ch 1, 7 dc in center st of next 5-dc group, ch 1**, dc in next dc, rep from * across, ending last rep at **, dc in 3rd ch of beg ch-4, turn.

Row 5: **Ch 3** *(see Pattern Notes)*, dc in same st, ch 2, dc in center st of next 7-dc group, ch 2, sk next 3 sts of same 7-dc group, [V-st in next st, ch 2, dc in center st of next 7-dc group, ch 2, sk next 3 sts of same 7-dc group] across, 2 dc in 3rd ch of beg ch-4, turn.

Row 6: Ch 3, dc in same st, ch 2, sk next st, dc in next dc, ch 2, [3 dc in ch sp of next V-st, ch 2, sk next st on same V-st, dc in next st, ch 2] across, 2 dc in 3rd ch of beg ch-3, turn.

Row 7: Ch 3, 2 dc in same st, ch 1, sk next st, dc in next st, ch 1, [5 dc in center st of next 3-dc group, ch 1, sk next st of same 3-dc group, dc in next st, ch 1] across, 3 dc in 3rd ch of beg ch-3, turn.

Row 8: Ch 3, 3 dc in same st, sk next 2 sts, dc in next st, [7 dc in center st of next 5-dc group, sk next 2 sts of same 5-dc group, dc in next st] across, 4 dc in 3rd ch of beg ch-3, turn.

Row 9: Ch 5, sk next 3 sts, V-st in next st, ch 2, [dc in center st of next 7-dc group, ch 2, sk next 3 sts of same 7-dc group, V-st in next st, ch 2] across, dc in 3rd ch of beg ch-3, turn.

Row 10: Ch 5, 3 dc in ch sp of next V-st, ch 2, dc in next dc, *ch 2, 3 dc in ch sp of next V-st, ch 2**, dc in next dc, rep from * across, ending last rep at **, dc in 5th ch of beg ch-5, turn.

Rep rows 3–10 for pattern, ending last rep with row 8. ■

Square 18

Multiple of 3 + 9

PATTERN NOTE
Chain-3 at beginning of row counts as first double crochet unless otherwise stated.

SPECIAL STITCHES
V-stitch (V-st): (Dc, ch 1, dc) in indicated place.

Shell: (2 dc, ch 1, 2 dc) in indicated place.

INSTRUCTIONS
SQUARE
Row 1 (RS): **V-st** (*see Special Stitches*) in 6th ch from hook (*first 5 chs count as first dc and sk 2 chs*), [sk next 2 chs, V-st in next ch] across to last 3 chs, sk next 2 chs, dc in last ch, turn.

Row 2: **Ch 3** (*see Pattern Note*), sk first st, **shell** (*see Special Stitches*) in ch sp of each V-st across, dc in 3rd ch of beg 5 sk chs, turn.

Row 3: Ch 3, sk first 3 sts, V-st in ch sp of each shell across, dc in 3rd ch of beg ch-3, turn.

Row 4: Ch 3, sk first st, shell in ch sp of each V-st across, dc in 3rd ch of beg ch-3, turn.

Rep rows 3 and 4 for pattern, ending last rep with row 3. ∎

Square 19

Multiple of 8 + 10

PATTERN NOTE
Chain-3 at beginning of row counts as first double crochet unless otherwise stated.

SPECIAL STITCH
V-stitch (V-st): (Dc, ch 1, dc) in indicated place.

INSTRUCTIONS
SQUARE
Row 1 (RS): Sc in 2nd ch from hook, [sk next 3 chs, 9 dc in next ch, sk next 3 chs, sc in next ch] across, turn.

Row 2: **Ch 3** (*see Pattern Note*), dc in same st, [ch 2, sc in center st of next 9-dc group, ch 2, **V-st** (*see Special Stitch*) in next sc] across to last 9-dc group, ch 2, sc in center st of next 9-dc group, ch 2, 2 dc in last st, turn.

Row 3: Ch 3, 4 dc in same st, sc in next sc, [9 dc in ch sp of next V-st, sc in next sc] across, 5 dc in 3rd ch of beg ch-3, turn.

Row 4: Ch 1, sc in first st, ch 2, V-st in next sc, [ch 2, sc in center st of next 9-dc group, ch 2, V-st in next sc] across, ch 2, sc in 3rd ch of beg ch-3, turn.

Row 5: Ch 1, sc in first st, [9 dc in ch sp of next V-st, sc in next sc] across, turn.

Rep rows 2–5 for pattern. ∎

Multiple of 8 + 1

PATTERN NOTE
Chain-3 at beginning of row counts as first double crochet unless otherwise stated.

INSTRUCTIONS
SQUARE
Row 1: Sc in 2nd ch from hook and in each ch across, turn.

Row 2 (RS): **Ch 3** *(see Pattern Note)*, [sk next st, 3 **fpdc** *(see Stitch Guide)* around next st, sk next st, dc in next st] across, turn.

Rnd 3: Ch 1, sc in each st across to last st, sc in 3rd ch of beg ch-3, turn.

Row 4: Ch 3, dc in same st, [sk next st, dc in next st, sk next st, 3 **fpdc** around next dc 2 rows below, sk next st 1 row below] across to last 4 sts, sk next st, dc in next st, sk next st, 2 dc in last st, turn.

Row 5: Ch 1, sc in each st across to last st, sc in 3rd ch of beg ch-3, turn.

Row 6: Ch 3, [sk next st, 3 fpdc around next dc 2 rows below, sk next st 1 row below, sk next st 1 row below, dc in next st] across, turn.

Row 7: Ch 1, sc in each st across to last st, sc in 3rd ch of beg ch-3, turn.

Rep rows 4–7 for pattern. ∎

Multiple of 2 + 6

PATTERN NOTE
This pattern is worked using a main color (MC) and contrasting color or colors (CC).

INSTRUCTIONS
SQUARE
Row 1 (RS): With MC, 2 dc in 4th ch from hook *(first 3 chs count as first dc)*, [sk next ch, 2 dc in next ch] across to last 2 chs, sk next ch, dc in last ch, **do not turn.** Fasten off.

Row 2: Join CC with sc in sp between first st and first 2-dc group, [ch 1, sc in sp between next 2 2-dc groups] across, ch 1, sc in sp between last 2-dc group and last st, **do not turn.** Fasten off.

Row 3: Join MC with sl st in first st of row before last, ch 3 *(counts as first dc)*, 2 dc in each ch-1 sp across last row, dc in last st on row before last, **do not turn**. Fasten off.

Rep rows 2 and 3 for pattern. ∎

Square 22

Multiple of 8 + 4

PATTERN NOTE
This pattern is worked using 3: colors A, B and C.

INSTRUCTIONS
SQUARE
Row 1 (RS): With A, 3 dc in 4th ch from hook *(first 3 chs count as first dc)*, [sk next 3 chs, 3 dc in next ch] across to last 4 chs, sk next 3 chs, dc in last ch, turn. Fasten off.

Row 2: Join B with sl st in first st, ch 3 *(counts as first dc)*, working over last row, 3 dc in 2nd of next 3 skipped chs on starting ch, [sk next 3 sts on previous row, working over previous row, 3 dc in 2nd of next 3 skipped chs on starting ch] across to last 3-dc group on previous row, sk next 3 sts, dc in 3rd ch of beg sk 3 chs, turn. Fasten off.

Row 3: Join C with sl st in first st, ch 3 *(counts as first dc)*, working over last row, 3 dc in center st

of first 3-dc group on 2nd row below, [sk next 3 sts on last row, working over last row, 3 dc in center st of next 3-dc group on 2nd row below] across to last 3-dc group on this row, sk next 3 sts, dc in 3rd ch of beg ch-3, turn. Fasten off.

Working in color sequence of A, B and C, rep row 3 for pattern. ∎

Square 23

Multiple of 6 + 10

PATTERN NOTES
This pattern is worked using a main color (MC) and contrasting color (CC).

Chain-3 at beginning of row counts as first double crochet unless otherwise stated.

INSTRUCTIONS
SQUARE
Row 1 (RS): With MC, 2 dc in 4th ch from hook *(first 3 chs count as first dc)*, [ch 3, sk next 5 chs, 5 dc in next ch] across to last 6 chs, ch 3, sk next 5 chs, 3 dc in last ch, **do not turn**. Fasten off.

Row 2: Join CC with sc in 3rd ch of beg sk 3 chs, *ch 2, working over next ch-3 sp, dc in 2nd ch of next 5 sk chs on starting ch, ch 1, working over same ch-3, dc in 4th sk ch of same 5 sk chs on starting ch, ch 2**, sc in center st of next 5-dc group on last row, rep from * across, ending last rep at **, dc in last st on last row, **do not turn**. Fasten off.

Row 3: Join MC with sc in first st, ch 1, 5 dc in next ch-1 sp, [ch 3, 5 dc in next ch-1 sp] across, ch 1, sc in last st, **do not turn**. Fasten off.

Row 4: Join CC with sl st in first st, **ch 3** (see Pattern Notes), working over next ch-1 sp, dc in next ch-2 sp on 2nd row below, ch 2, sc in center st of next 5-dc group on last row, [ch 2, working over next ch-3 sp, dc in next ch-2 sp on 2nd row below, ch 1, working over same ch-3 sp, dc in next ch-2 sp on 2nd row below, ch 2, sc in center st of next 5-dc group on last row] across, ch 2, working over next ch-1 sp, dc in next ch-2 sp on 2nd row below, dc in last st on last row, **do not turn**. Fasten off.

Row 5: Join MC with sl st in 3rd ch of beg ch-3, ch 3, 2 dc in same st, (ch 3, 5 dc) in each ch-1 sp across, ch 3, 3 dc in last st, **do not turn**. Fasten off.

Row 6: Join CC with sc in 3rd ch of beg ch-3, *ch 2, working over next ch-3 sp, dc in next ch-2 sp on 2nd row below, ch 1, working over same ch-3, dc in next ch-2 sp on 2nd row below, ch 2**, sc in center st of next 5-dc group on last row, rep from * across, ending last rep at **, sc in last st on last row, **do not turn**. Fasten off.

Row 7: Join MC with sc in first st, ch 1, 5 dc in next ch-1 sp, [ch 3, 5 dc in next ch-1 sp] across, ch 1, sc in last st, **do not turn**. Fasten off.

Row 8: Join CC with sl st in first st, ch 3, working over next ch-1 sp, dc in next ch-2 sp on 2nd row below, ch 2, sc in center st of next 5-dc group on last row, [ch 2, working over next ch-3 sp, dc in next ch-2 sp on 2nd row below, ch 1, working over same ch-3 sp, dc in next ch-2 sp on 2nd row below, ch 2, sc in center st of next 5-dc group on last row] across , ch 2, working over next ch-1 sp, dc in next ch-2 sp on 2nd row below, dc in last st on last row, **do not turn**. Fasten off.

Rep rows 5–8 for pattern. ∎

Square 24

Multiple of 4 + 5

PATTERN NOTES
This pattern is worked using 2 colors A and B.

Chain-3 at beginning of row counts as first double crochet unless otherwise stated.

Chain-4 at beginning of row counts as first double crochet and ch-1 space unless otherwise stated.

INSTRUCTIONS
SQUARE
Row 1 (RS): With A, dc in 4th ch from hook (first 3 chs count as first dc), dc in next ch, [ch 1, sk next ch, dc in each of next 3 chs] across, turn.

Row 2: **Ch 3** (see Pattern Notes), sk first st, dc in each of next 2 sts, *ch 1, sk next ch sp**, dc in each of next 3 sts, rep from * across, ending last rep at **, dc in each of next 3 sts, dc in 3rd ch of beg 3 sk chs, turn. Fasten off.

Row 3: Join B with sl st in first st, **ch 4** (see Pattern Notes), sk next st, [dc next st, working over ch-1 sp in last row, dc in next ch-1 sp 2 rows below, dc in next st on last row, ch 1, sk next st] across to last st, dc in 3rd ch of beg ch-3, turn.

Row 4: Ch 4, sk first st and next ch sp, [dc in each of next 3 sts, ch 1, sk next ch sp] across to last st, dc in 3rd ch of beg ch-4, turn. Fasten off.

Row 5: Join A with sl st in first st, ch 3, sk first st, working over ch-1 sp in last row, dc in next ch-1 sp 2 rows below, dc in next st on last row, *ch 1, sk next st, dc in next st, working over ch-1 sp in last row, dc in next ch-1 sp 2 rows below**, dc in next st on last row, rep from * across, ending last rep at **, dc in 3rd ch of beg ch-4, turn.

Row 6: Ch 3, sk first st, dc in each of next 2 sts, *ch 1, sk next ch sp**, dc in each of next 3 sts, across, ending last rep at **, dc in each of next 2 sts, dc in 3rd ch of beg ch-3, turn. Fasten off.

Rep rows 3–6 for pattern. ∎

Multiple of 12 + 2

PATTERN NOTES
This pattern is worked using 2 colors A and B.

Chain-3 at beginning of row counts as first double crochet unless otherwise stated.

SPECIAL STITCH
Cross-stitch (cross-st): Dc in sp after next sc on row before last, ch 1, dc in sp before same sc.

INSTRUCTIONS
SQUARE
Row 1 (RS): With A, sc in 2nd ch from hook, [sk next 2 chs, 5 dc in next ch, sk next 2 chs, sc in next ch] across, turn. Fasten off.

Row 2: Join B with sl st in first st, **ch 3** *(see Pattern Notes)*, dc in same st, ch 1, sc in center st of next 5-dc group, ch 1, [working on next sc on last row, **cross-st** *(see Special Stitch)*, ch 1, sc in center st of next 5-dc group, ch 1] across, 2 dc in last st, turn.

Row 3: Ch 3, 2 dc in same st, sc in next sc, [5 dc in ch-1 sp in center of next cross-st, sc in next sc] across, 3 dc in 3rd ch of beg ch-3, turn. Fasten off.

Row 4: Join A with sc in first st, ch 1, cross-st, ch 1, [sc in center st of next 5-dc group, ch 1, cross-st, ch 1] across, sc in 3rd ch of beg ch-3, turn.

Row 5: Ch 1, sc in first st, 5 dc in ch sp at center of next cross-st, [sc in next sc, 5 dc in ch at center of next cross st] across, sc in last st, turn. Fasten off.

Row 6: Join B with sl st in first st, ch 3, dc in same st, ch 1, sc in center st of next 5-dc group, ch 1, [cross-st, ch 1, sc in center st of next 5-dc group, ch 1] across, 2 dc in last st, turn.

Row 7: Ch 3, 2 dc in same st, sc in next sc, [5 dc in ch-1 sp in center of next cross-st, sc in next sc] across, 3 dc in 3rd ch of beg ch-3, turn. Fasten off.

Rep rows 4–7 for pattern. ∎

Multiple of 12 + 15

PATTERN NOTES

This pattern is worked using 2 colors A and B.

Chain-3 at beginning of row counts as first double crochet unless otherwise stated.

SPECIAL STITCH

Cross-stitch (cross-st): Fpdc *(see Stitch Guide)* around 4th st of same 5-dc group, ch 1, dc around 2nd st of same 5-dc group.

INSTRUCTIONS
SQUARE

Row 1: With A, dc in 4th ch from hook *(first 3 chs count as first dc)*, dc in next ch, ch 1, sk next 3 chs, 5 dc in next ch, ch 1, sk next 3 chs, [dc in each of next 5 chs, ch 1, sk next 3 chs, 5 dc in next ch, ch 1, sk next 3 chs] across to last 3 chs, dc in each of last 3 chs, turn. Fasten off.

Row 2 (RS): Join B with sl st in first st, **ch 3** *(see Pattern Notes)*, dc in each of next 2 sts, ch 1, dc in first st of next 5-dc group, **cross-st** *(see Special Stitch)*, dc in last st of same 5-dc group, ch 1, [dc in each of next 5 sts, ch 1, dc in first st of next 5-dc group, cross-st, dc in last st of same 5-dc group, ch 1] across to last 3 sts, dc in each of next 2 sts, dc in 3rd ch of beg sk 3 chs, turn. Fasten off.

Row 3: Join A with sl st in first st, ch 3, dc in each of next 2 sts, ch 1, 5 dc in ch sp at center of next cross-st, ch 1, [dc in each of next 5 sts, ch 1, 5 dc in ch sp at center of next cross-st, ch 1] across to last 3 sts, dc in each of next 2 sts, dc in 3rd ch of beg ch-3, turn. Fasten off.

Row 4: Join B with sl st in first st, ch 3, dc in each of next 2 sts, ch 1, dc in first st of next 5-dc group, cross-st, dc in last st of same 5-dc group, ch 1, [dc in each of next 5 sts, ch 1, dc in first st of next 5-dc group, cross-st, dc in last st of same 5-dc group, ch 1] across to last 3 sts, dc in each of next 2 sts, dc in 3rd ch of beg ch-3, turn. Fasten off.

Rep rows 3 and 4 for pattern, ending last rep with row 3. ∎

Square 27

Multiple of 8 + 4

PATTERN NOTE

Chain-3 at beginning of row counts as first double crochet unless otherwise stated.

SPECIAL STITCHES

Long double crochet (long dc): Yo, insert hook in indicated place on row before last, yo, pull up long lp, complete as dc.

Shell: (2 dc, ch 2, 2 dc) in indicated place.

V-stitch (V-st): (Dc, ch 2, dc) in indicated place.

INSTRUCTIONS
SQUARE

Row 1 (RS): **Shell** *(see Special Stitches)* in 5th ch from hook *(first 4 chs count as first dc and first sk ch)*, [sk next 3 chs, shell in next ch] across to last 3 chs, sk next 2 chs, dc in last ch, turn.

Row 2: **Ch 3** *(see Pattern Note)*, sk first st, [**long dc** *(see Special Stitches)* in same ch as next shell, **V-st** *(see Special Stitches)* in ch-2 sp of same shell, long dc in same ch as previous long dc] across, dc in 3rd ch of beg 4 sk chs, turn.

Row 3: Ch 3, sk first st, [long dc same ch-2 sp as next V-st, V-st in ch-2 sp of same V-st on last row, long dc in same ch-2 sp as last long dc] across, dc in 3rd ch of beg ch-3, turn.

Rep row 3 for pattern. ∎

Square 28

Multiple of 6 + 2

PATTERN NOTE

Chain-3 at beginning of row counts as first double crochet unless otherwise stated.

SPECIAL STITCH

Puff stitch (puff st): Yo, insert hook in indicated st, yo, pull lp through, [yo, insert hook in same st, yo, pull lp through] twice, yo, pull through all 7 lps on hook.

INSTRUCTIONS

SQUARE

Row 1: Sc in 2nd ch from hook, [ch 2, sk next 2 chs, sc in next ch] across, turn.

Row 2 (RS): **Ch 3** (see Pattern Note), sk first st, **puff st** (see Special Stitch) in next ch sp, [ch 1, 3 dc in next ch sp, ch 1, puff st in next ch sp] across to last ch sp, ch 1, 3 dc in last ch sp, ch 1, dc in last st, turn.

Row 3: Ch 1, sk first st, sc in first ch sp, [ch 3, sc in next ch-1 sp] across, ch 3, sc in 3rd ch of beg ch-3, turn.

Row 4: Ch 3, sk first st, 3 dc in next ch sp, [ch 1, puff st in next ch sp, ch 1, 3 dc in next ch sp] across to last ch sp, ch 1, puff st in last ch sp, ch 1, dc in last st, turn.

Row 5: Ch 1, sk first st, sc in first ch sp, [ch 3, sc in next ch-1 sp] across, ch 3, sc in 3rd ch of beg ch-3, turn.

Rep rows 2–5 for pattern, ending with row 4. ∎

Square 29

Multiple of 8 + 6

SPECIAL STITCH

Cross-stitch (cross-st): Sk next 2 chs or sts, dc in each of next 2 chs or sts, working in front of 2 dc just made, dc in each of 2 sk chs or sts.

INSTRUCTIONS

SQUARE

Row 1 (RS): Dc in 4th ch from hook (first 3 chs count as first dc), dc in each of next 2 chs, [**cross-st** (see Special Stitch), dc in each of next 4 chs] across, turn.

Row 2: Ch 3 (counts as first dc), sk first st, dc in each of next 3 sts, *cross-st**, dc in each of next 4 sts, rep from * across to last 4 sts, ending last rep at **, dc in each of next 3 sts, dc in 3rd ch of beg sk 3 chs, turn.

Row 3: Ch 3, sk first st, dc in each of next 3 sts, *cross-st**, dc in each of next 4 sts, rep from * across to last 4 sts, ending last rep at **, dc in each of next 3 sts, dc in 3rd ch of beg ch-3, turn.

Rep row 3 for pattern. ■

Square 30

Multiple of 6 + 7

PATTERN NOTE
Chain-3 at beginning of row counts as first double crochet unless otherwise stated.

SPECIAL STITCH
Puff stitch (puff st): Yo, insert hook in indicated st, yo, pull lp through, [yo, insert hook in same st, yo, pull lp through] twice, yo, pull through all 7 lps on hook.

INSTRUCTIONS
SQUARE
Row 1 (RS): Dc in 6th ch from hook (*first 5 chs count as first dc and ch-2 sp*), *ch 2, working over last dc made, dc in 3rd ch before last dc**, dc in each of next 2 chs, sk next 3 chs, dc in next ch, rep from * across, ending last rep at **, dc in last ch, turn.

Row 2: Ch 4 (*counts as first dc and ch-1 sp*), **puff st** (*see Special Stitch*) in next ch-2 sp, ch 1, [dc in sp after next 2-dc group, ch 2, dc in sp before

same 2-dc group, ch 1, puff st in next ch-2 sp, ch 1] across to last st, dc in 3rd ch of beg 6 sk chs, turn.

Row 3: Ch 3, dc in sp after next puff st, ch 2, dc in sp before same puff st, [2 dc in next ch-2 sp, dc in sp after next puff st, ch 2, dc in sp before same puff st] across to last st, dc in 3rd ch of beg ch-4, turn.

Row 4: Ch 4 (*counts as first dc and ch-1 sp*), puff st in next ch-2 sp, ch 1, [dc in sp after next 2-dc group, ch 2, dc in sp before same 2-dc group, ch 1, puff st in next ch-2 sp, ch 1] across to last st, dc in 3rd ch of ch-3, turn.

Rep rows 3 and 4 for pattern, ending last rep with row 3. ■

Square 31

Multiple of 8 + 10

PATTERN NOTE
Chain-3 at beginning of row counts as first double crochet unless otherwise stated.

INSTRUCTIONS
SQUARE
Row 1 (RS): Sc in 2nd ch from hook, [sk next 3 chs, 9 dc in next ch, sk next 3 chs, sc in next ch] across, turn.

Row 2: Ch 6 *(counts as first dc and ch-3 sp)*, sc in 5th st of next 9-dc group, ch 3, [dc in next sc, ch 3, sc in 5th st of next 9-dc group, ch 3] across to last st, dc in last st, turn.

Row 3: **Ch 3** *(see Pattern Note)*, sk first st, 3 dc in next ch sp, [ch 1, 3 dc in next ch-3 sp] across to last st, dc in 3rd ch of beg ch-6, turn.

Row 4: Ch 3, sk first st, dc in each of next 3 sts, [ch 1, dc in each of next 3 sts] across to last st, dc in 3rd ch of beg ch-3, turn.

Row 5: Ch 1, sc in first st, 9 dc in next ch-sp, [sc in next ch-1 sp, 9 dc in next ch-1 sp] across, sc in 3rd ch of beg ch-3, turn.

Rep rows 2–5 for pattern. ∎

Square 32

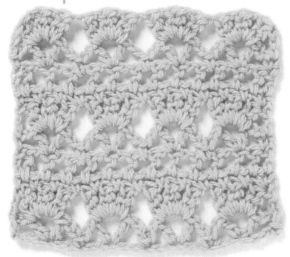

Multiple of 6 + 8

SPECIAL STITCHES
V-stitch (V-st): (Dc, ch 2, dc) in indicated place.

Cluster (cl): Yo, insert hook in next ch sp, yo, pull lp through, yo, pull through 2 lps on hook, yo, insert hook in same ch sp, yo, pull lp through, yo, pull through 2 lps on hook, yo, pull through all 3 lps on hook.

PATTERN NOTE
Chain-3 at beginning of row counts as first double crochet unless otherwise stated.

INSTRUCTIONS
SQUARE
Row 1 (RS): Sc in 2nd ch from hook, [ch 2, sk next 2 chs, **V-st** *(see Special Stitches)* in next ch, ch 2, sk next 2 chs, sc in next ch] across, turn.

Row 2: **Ch 3** *(see Pattern Note)*, [(**cl**—*see Special Stitches*, {ch 1, cl} twice) in ch sp of next V-st, ch 1] across to last V-st, (cl, {ch 1, cl} twice) in ch sp of last V-st, dc in last st, turn.

Row 3: Ch 1, sc in first st, [ch 1, sc in next ch-sp] across to last st, ch 1, sc in 3rd ch of beg ch-3, turn.

Row 4: Ch 3, dc in first ch-1 sp, [ch 1, dc in next ch-1 sp] across to last st, dc in last st, turn.

Row 5: Ch 1, sc in first st, ch 2, sk next dc, V-st in next dc, [ch 2, sk next dc, sc in next ch sp, ch 2, sk next dc, V-st in next st] across to last 2 sts, ch 2, sk next st, sc in 3rd ch of beg ch-3, turn.

Rep rows 2–5 for pattern, ending with row 2. ∎

Square 33

Multiple of 4 + 6

SPECIAL STITCH
Puff stitch (puff st): Yo, insert hook in indicated st, yo, pull lp through, yo, insert hook in same st, yo, pull lp through, yo, pull through all 5 lps on hook.

INSTRUCTIONS
SQUARE
Row 1 (RS): Sc in 2nd ch from hook, [ch 2, sk next ch, **puff st** (see Special Stitch) in next ch, ch 2, sk next ch, sc in next ch] across, turn.

Row 2: Ch 5 (counts as first dc and ch-2 sp), sc in next puff st, [ch 5, sc in next puff st] across to last st, ch 2, dc in last st, turn.

Row 3: Ch 1, sc in first st, ch 2, puff st in next sc, [ch 2, sc in next ch-5 sp, ch 2, puff st in next sc] across to last st, ch 2, sc in 3rd ch of beg ch-5, turn.

Rep rows 2 and 3 for pattern. ■

Square 34

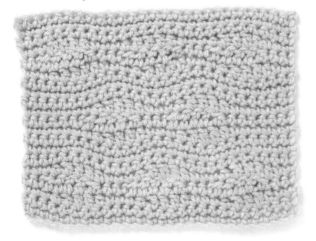

Multiple of 8 + 3

INSTRUCTIONS
SQUARE
Row 1 (RS): Sc in 2nd ch from hook and in each ch across, turn.

Row 2: Ch 1, sc in each st across, turn.

Rows 3–5: Ch 1, sc in each of first 2 sts, [hdc in next st, dc in each of next 3 sts, hdc in next st, sc in each of next 3 sts] across.

Rows 6–8: Ch 1, sc in each st across, turn.

Rows 9–11: Ch 1, sc in each of first 6 sts, [hdc in next st, dc in each of next 3 sts, hdc in next st, sc in each of next 3 sts] across to last 4 sts, sc in each of last 4 sts, turn.

Rows 12–14: Ch 1, sc in each st across, turn.

Rep rows 3–14 for pattern, ending last rep with row 8. ■

Square 35

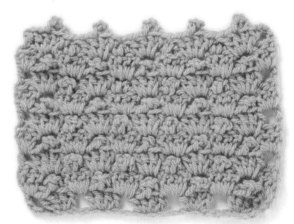

Multiple of 12 + 4

PATTERN NOTE
Chain-3 at beginning of row counts as first double crochet unless otherwise stated.

SPECIAL STITCHES
Picot: Ch 3, sl st in top of last st made.

Shell: (2 dc, **picot**—see Special Stitches, 2 dc) in indicated place.

INSTRUCTIONS
SQUARE
Row 1 (RS): **Shell** (see Special Stitches) in 5th ch from hook (first 4 chs count as first dc and

sp between shell and st), [sk next 3 chs, shell in next ch] across to last 3 chs, sk next 2 chs, dc in last ch, turn.

Row 2: **Ch 3** *(see Pattern Note)*, sk first st, 2 dc in sp between first st and first shell, [shell in sp between next 2 shells] across to last shell, 2 dc in sp between last shell and last st, dc in 3rd ch of beg 4 sk chs, turn.

Row 3: Ch 3, shell in sp between first 3 sts and next shell, [shell in sp between next 2 shells] across to last shell, shell in sp between last shell and last 3 dc, dc in 3rd ch of beg ch-3, turn.

Row 4: Ch 3, sk first st, 2 dc in sp between first st and first shell, [shell in sp between next 2 shells] across to last shell, 2 dc in sp between last shell and last st, dc in 3rd ch of beg ch-3, turn.

Rep rows 3 and 4 for pattern, ending last rep with row 3. ■

Square 36

Multiple of 8 + 9

PATTERN NOTES

Chain-2 at beginning of row counts as first half double crochet unless otherwise stated.

Skip stitch on previous row behind each front post treble crochet.

SPECIAL STITCH

Popcorn (pc): 5 hdc in indicated st, drop lp from hook, insert hook in top of first st of 5-hdc group, pull dropped lp through.

INSTRUCTIONS
SQUARE

Row 1 (RS): Hdc in 3rd ch from hook and in each ch across, turn.

Row 2: **Ch 2** *(see Pattern Notes)*, hdc in each st across to last st, hdc in 2nd ch of beg sk 2 chs, turn.

Row 3: Ch 2, sk next 2 sts on previous row, ***fptr** (see Stitch Guide) around 4th st 2 rows below, **sk 3rd st on previous row** (see Pattern Notes), hdc in next st on previous row, **pc** (see Special Stitch) in next st, hdc in next st, fptr around same st 2 rows below as last post st, sk next st on previous row **, hdc in each of next 3 sts on previous row, sk next 7 sts 2 rows below, rep from * across, ending last rep at **, hdc in 2nd ch of beg ch-2, turn.

Row 4: Ch 2, hdc in each st across to last st, hdc in 2nd ch of beg ch-2, turn.

Row 5: Ch 2, sk first st, hdc in each of next 4 sts, [fptr around center st of next 3-hdc group 2 rows below, sk next st on previous row, hdc in next st, pc in next st, hdc in next st, fptr around same st 2 rows below as last post st, sk next st on previous row, hdc in each of next 3 sts] across to last 2 sts, hdc in next st, hdc in 2nd ch of beg ch-2, turn.

Row 6: Ch 2, hdc in each st across to last st, hdc in 2nd ch of beg ch-2, turn.

Row 7: Ch 2, sk first 2 sts on previous row, fptr around 4th st 2 rows below, sk next st on previous row, hdc in next st on previous row, pc in next st, hdc in next st, fptr around same st 2 rows below as last post st, sk next st on previous row, *hdc in each of next 3 sts, fptr about center st of next 3-hdc group on row before last, hdc in next st, pc in next st, hdc in next st, fptr around same st on row before last as last post st**, hdc in each of next 3 sts, sk next 7 sts 2 rows below rep from * across to last st, hdc in 2nd ch of beg ch-2, turn.

Rep rows 4–7 for pattern, ending with row 5. ■

Square 37

Multiple of 5 + 4

PATTERN NOTES
Chain-3 at beginning of row counts as first double crochet unless otherwise stated.

Skip stitches on last row behind post stitches.

SPECIAL STITCH
Popcorn (pc): 5 dc in indicated st, drop lp from hook, insert hook in top of first st of 5-dc group, pull dropped lp through.

INSTRUCTIONS
SQUARE
Row 1 (RS): Dc in 4th ch from hook (*first 3 chs count as first dc*) and in each ch across, turn.

Row 2: Ch 1, sc in each st across to last st, sc in 3rd ch of beg 3 sk chs, turn.

Row 3: Ch 3 (*see Pattern Notes*), sk first st, dc in next st, *sk next 2 sts, **fpdc** (*see Stitch Guide*) around 5th st 2 rows below, dc in 2nd sk st on previous row, fpdc around 3rd st 2 rows below, dc in each of next 2 sts on previous row, rep from * across, turn.

Row 4: Ch 1, sc in each st across to last st, sc in 3rd ch of beg ch-3, turn.

Row 5: Ch 3, sk first st, dc in next st, [fpdc around next post st 2 rows below, **pc** (*see Special Stitch*) in next dc on previous row, fpdc around next post st 2 rows below, dc in each of next 2 sts on previous row] across, turn.

Row 6: Ch 1, sc in each st across, turn.

Row 7: Ch 3, sk first st, dc in next st, [sk next post st 2 rows below, fpdc around next post st, working behind last post st, dc in next st on previous row, working in front of last post st, fpdc around sk post st 2 rows below, dc in each of next 2 sts on last row] across, turn.

Rep rows 4–7 for pattern. ■

Square 38

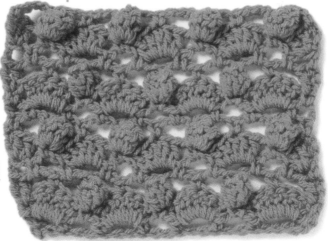

Multiple of 6 + 7

PATTERN NOTES
Chain-3 at beginning of row counts as first double crochet unless otherwise stated.

Chain-4 at beginning of row counts as first hdc and chain-1 space unless otherwise stated.

SPECIAL STITCHES
Front popcorn (front pc): 5 dc in indicated st, drop lp from hook, insert hook from front to back through top of first st of 5-dc group, pick up dropped lp, pull dropped lp through.

Back popcorn (back pc): 5 dc in indicated st, drop lp from hook, insert hook from back to front, through top of first st of 5-dc group, pick up dropped lp, pull dropped lp through.

Shell: 5 dc in indicated st.

INSTRUCTIONS
SQUARE
Row 1 (RS): Sc in 5th ch from hook (*first 4 chs count as first hdc and ch-1 sp*), [ch 3, sk next 2 chs, sc in next ch] across to last 2 chs, ch 3, sk next ch, hdc in last ch, turn.

Row 2: Ch 1, sc in first st, *ch 1, **shell** (*see Special Stitches*) in next ch-3 sp, ch 1, sc in next ch sp, rep from * across to last 2 sts, ch 1, sk next st, sc in 3rd ch of beg 4 sk chs, turn.

Row 3: **Ch 3** (*see Pattern Notes*), dc in same st, [ch 3, sc in center st of next shell, ch 3, **front pc** (*see Special Stitches*) in next sc] across to last shell, ch 3, sc in center st of next shell, ch 3, 2 dc in last st, turn.

Row 4: **Ch 4** (*see Pattern Notes*), sc in next ch-3 sp, [ch 3, sc in next ch-3 sp] across, ch 1, hdc in 3rd ch of beg ch-3, turn.

Row 5: Ch 3, 2 dc in next ch-1 sp, [ch 1, sc in next ch-3 sp, ch 1, shell in next ch-3 sp] across to last ch-3 sp, ch 1, sc in last ch-3 sp, ch 1, 3 dc in 3rd ch of beg ch-4, turn.

Row 6: Ch 1, sc in first st, [ch 3, **back pc** (*see Special Stitches*) in next sc, ch 3, sc in center st of next shell] across to last sc, ch 3, back pc in last sc, ch 3, sk next 2 sts, sc in 3rd ch of beg ch-3, turn.

Row 7: Ch 4, sc in next ch-3 sp, [ch 3, sc in next ch-3 sp] across to last st, ch 1, hdc in last st, turn.

Row 8: Ch 1, sc in first st, *ch 1, shell in next ch-3 sp, ch 1, sc in next ch sp, rep from * across to last 2 sts, ch 1, sk next st, sc in 3rd ch of beg ch-4, turn.

Rep rows 3–8 for pattern, ending with row 7. ∎

Square 39

Multiple of 4 + 3

PATTERN NOTES
This pattern is worked using 2 colors A and B.

Chain-3 at beginning of row counts as first double crochet unless otherwise stated.

SPECIAL STITCHES
Front popcorn (front pc): 5 dc in indicated st, drop lp from hook, insert hook from front to back through top of first st of 5-dc group, pull dropped lp through.

Back popcorn (back pc): 5 dc in indicated st, drop lp from hook, insert hook from back to front, through top of first st of 5-dc group, pull dropped lp through.

V-stitch (V-st): (Dc, ch 3, dc) in indicated st.

INSTRUCTIONS
SQUARE
Row 1 (RS): With A, sc in 2nd ch from hook, ch 3, **front pc** (*see Special Stitches*) in same ch, [sk next 3 chs, (sc, ch 3, front pc) in next ch] across to last ch, sc in last ch, turn.

Row 2: **Ch 3** (*see Pattern Notes*), 2 dc in same st, (sc, ch 3, **back pc**—*see Special Stitches*) in each ch-3 sp across to last ch-3 sp, sc in last ch-3 sp, ch 2, dc in last st, turn. Fasten off.

Row 3: Join B with sc in first st, **V-st** (*see Special Stitches*) in next sc, [sc in next ch-3 sp, V-st in next sc] across, sc in 3rd ch of beg ch-3, turn.

Row 4: Ch 6 (*counts as first dc and ch-3 sp*), sc in ch sp of next V-st, [ch 3, sc in ch sp of next V-st] across, ch 3, dc in last st, turn. Fasten off.

Row 5: Join A with sc in first st, ch 3, front pc in same st, (sc, ch 3, front pc) in each sc across to last st, sc in 3rd ch of beg ch-6, turn.

Rep rows 2–5 for pattern. ■

Row 2: Ch 3 (*counts as first dc*), 2 dc same st, *ch 1, sk next st, dc in next st, ch 1, dc in next st, ch 1, cl dec, (ch 1, dc in next st) twice, ch 1**, shell in ch sp of next shell, rep from * across, ending last rep at **, 3 dc in 3rd ch of beg sk 3 chs, turn.

Row 3: Ch 3, 2 dc same st, *ch 1, sk next st, dc in next st, ch 1, dc in next st, ch 1, cl dec, (ch 1, dc in next st) twice, ch 1**, shell in ch sp of next shell, rep from * across, ending last rep at **, 3 dc in 3rd ch of beg ch-3, turn.

Rep row 3 for pattern. ■

Square 40

Multiple of 16 + 20

SPECIAL STITCHES
Cluster decrease (cl dec): Yo, insert hook in next st or ch, yo, pull lp through, yo, pull through 2 lps on hook, [sk next st or ch, yo, insert hook in next st or ch, yo, pull lp through, yo, pull through 2 lps on hook] twice, yo, pull through all 4 lps on hook.

Shell: (2 dc, ch 1, 2 dc) in next ch or st.

INSTRUCTIONS
SQUARE
Row 1 (RS): 2 dc in 4th ch from hook (*first 3 chs count as first dc*), *(ch 1, sk next ch, dc in next ch) twice, ch 1, sk next ch, **cl dec** (*see Special Stitches*), (ch 1, sk next ch, dc in next ch) twice, ch 1, sk next ch**, **shell** (*see Special Stitches*) in next ch, rep from * across, ending last rep at **, 3 dc in last ch, turn.

Square 41

Multiple of 8 + 11

PATTERN NOTE
Chain-3 at beginning of row counts as first double crochet unless otherwise stated.

INSTRUCTIONS
SQUARE
Row 1 (RS): Dc in 4th ch from hook (*first 3 chs count as first dc*), *ch 3, sk next 2 chs, sc in next ch, ch 3, sk next 2 chs**, dc in each of next 3 chs, rep from * across, ending last rep at **, dc in each of last 2 chs, turn.

Row 2: **Ch 3** (*see Pattern Note*), sk first st, *dc in next dc, dc in next ch-3 sp, ch 3, dc in next ch-3 sp, dc in next dc**, **bpdc** (*see Stitch Guide*) around next dc, rep from * across, ending last rep at **, dc in 3rd ch of beg sk 3 chs, turn.

Row 3: Ch 3, sk first st, *dc in next dc, ch 3, sc in next ch-3 sp, ch 3, sk next dc, dc in next st**, **fpdc** (*see Stitch Guide*) in next st, rep from * across, ending last rep at **, dc in 3rd ch of beg ch-3, turn.

Row 4: Ch 3, sk first st, *dc in next dc, dc in next ch-3 sp, ch 3, dc in next ch-3 sp, dc in next dc**, bpdc around next dc, rep from * across, ending last rep at **, dc in 3rd ch of beg ch-3, turn.

Rep rows 3 and 4 for pattern, ending last rep with row 3. ∎

Square 42

Multiple of 8 + 12

SPECIAL STITCHES
Puff stitch (puff st): Yo, insert hook in indicated st, yo, pull lp through, [yo, insert hook in same st, yo, pull lp through] twice, yo, pull through all 7 lps on hook.

Shell: (3 dc, ch 1, 3 dc) in indicated place.

INSTRUCTIONS
SQUARE
Row 1 (RS): 2 dc in 4th ch from hook (*first 3 chs count as first dc*), *ch 1, sk next 3 chs, sc in next ch, ch 1, sk next 3 chs**, **shell** (*see Special Stitches*) in next ch, rep from * across, ending last rep at **, 3 dc in last ch, turn.

Row 2: Ch 1, sc in first st, *ch 3, **puff st** (*see Special Stitches*) in next sc, ch 3**, sc in ch sp of next shell, rep from * across, ending last rep at **, sc in 3rd ch of beg 3 sk chs, turn.

Row 3: Ch 1, sc in first st, [ch 1, shell in next puff st, ch 1, sc in next sc] across, turn.

Row 4: Ch 6 (*counts as first dc and ch-3 sp*), sc in ch sp of next shell, [ch 3, puff st in next sc, ch 3, sc in ch sp of next shell] across to last st, ch 3, dc in last st, turn.

Row 5: Ch 3, 2 dc in same st, ch 1, sc in next sc, [ch 1, shell in next puff st, ch 1, sc in next sc] across to last st, ch 1, 3 dc in last 3rd ch of beg ch-6, turn.

Row 6: Ch 1, sc in first st, *ch 3, puff st in next sc, ch 3**, sc in ch sp of next shell, rep from * across, ending last rep at **, sc in 3rd ch of beg ch-3, turn.

Rep rows 3–6 for pattern, ending with row 5. ∎

Square 43

Multiple of 10 + 11

PATTERN NOTE
Chain-3 at beginning of row counts as first double crochet unless otherwise stated.

SPECIAL STITCHES
Front popcorn (front pc): 5 dc in indicated st, drop lp from hook, insert hook from front to back through top of first st of 5-dc group, pull dropped lp through.

Back popcorn (back pc): 5 dc in indicated st, drop lp from hook, insert hook from back to front, through top of first st of 5-dc group, pull dropped lp through.

INSTRUCTIONS
SQUARE
Row 1 (RS): Dc in 4th ch from hook (*first 3 chs count as first dc*), *sk next ch, (**front pc**—*see Special Stitches*, ch 3, dc) in next ch, sk next 3 chs**, dc in each of next 5 chs, rep from * across, ending last rep at **, dc in each of last 2 chs, turn.

Row 2: Ch 3 (*see Pattern Note*), sk first st, dc in next st, *(**back pc**—*see Special Stitches*, ch 3, dc) in next ch-3 sp**, dc in each of next 5 sts, rep from * across, ending last rep at **, sk next pc, dc in last dc and in 3rd ch of beg 3 sk chs, turn.

Row 3: Ch 3, sk first st, dc in next st, *(front pc, ch 3, dc) in next ch-3 sp**, dc in each of next 5 sts, rep from * across, ending last rep at **, sk last pc, dc in last dc and in 3rd ch of beg ch-3, turn.

Row 4: Ch 3, sk first st, dc in next st, *(back pc, ch 3, dc) in next ch-3 sp**, dc in each of next 5 sts, rep from * across, ending last rep at **, sk next pc, dc in last dc and in 3rd ch of beg ch-3, turn.

Rep rows 3 and 4 for pattern, ending last rep with row 3. ∎

Square 44

Multiple of 3 + 5

PATTERN NOTES
Chain-3 at beginning of row counts as first double crochet unless otherwise stated.

Chain-4 at beginning of row counts as first double crochet and chain-1 unless otherwise stated.

SPECIAL STITCH
Popcorn (pc): 5 dc in indicated place, drop lp from hook, insert hook in top of first st of 5-dc group, pull dropped lp through.

INSTRUCTIONS
SQUARE
Row 1 (RS): Sc in 2nd ch from hook and in each ch across, turn.

Row 2: Ch 1, sc in first st, [ch 3, sk next 2 sts, sc in next st] across, turn.

Row 3: Ch 4 (*see Pattern Notes*), sk first st, **pc** (*see Special Stitch*) in next ch sp, [ch 2, pc in next ch sp] across, ch 1, dc in last st, turn.

Row 4: Ch 1, sc in first st, sc in next ch-1 sp, sc in top of each pc and 2 sc in each ch-2 sp across to last st, sc in 3rd ch of beg ch-4, turn.

Row 5: Ch 3 (*see Pattern Notes*), sk first 2 sts, [**fpdc** (*see Stitch Guide*) around next pc 2 rows below, sk next st on previous row behind post st, dc in each of next 2 sts on previous row] across, turn.

Row 6: Ch 3, sk first st, dc in next st, **bpdc** (*see Stitch Guide*) around fpdc, [dc in each of next 2 sts, bpdc around next fpdc] across to last st, dc in 3rd ch of beg ch-3, turn.

Row 7: Ch 3, sk first st, *fpdc around next bpdc**, dc in each of next 2 sts, rep from * across, ending last rep at **, dc in next st, dc in 3rd ch of beg ch-3, turn.

Rep rows 2–7 for pattern. ∎

Square 45

Multiple of 8 + 12

PATTERN NOTE
This pattern is worked using 2 colors A and B.

SPECIAL STITCH
Shell: (2 dc, ch 1, 2 dc) in indicated place.

INSTRUCTIONS
SQUARE
Row 1 (RS): With A, 2 dc in 4th ch from hook (*first 3 chs count as first dc*), *ch 3, sk next 7 chs**, **shell** (*see Special Stitch*) in next ch, rep from * across, ending last rep at **, 3 dc in last ch, **do not turn**. Fasten off.

Row 2: Join B with sc in first st, ch 1, *working over ch-3, shell in 4th ch of next 7 sk chs of starting ch**, ch 3, rep from * across, ending last rep at **, ch 1, sc in last st, **do not turn**. Fasten off.

Row 3: Join A with sl st in first st, ch 3 (*counts as first dc*), 2 dc in same st, *ch 3, sk next shell**, working over next ch-3, shell in ch sp of next shell on row before last, rep from * across, ending last rep at **, 3 dc in last st, **do not turn**. Fasten off.

Row 4: Join B with sc in first st, ch 1, *working over next ch-3, shell in ch sp of next shell on row before last**, ch 3, sk next shell, rep from *, ending last rep at **, ch 1, sc in last st, **do not turn**.

Rep rows 3 and 4 for pattern. ∎

Square 46

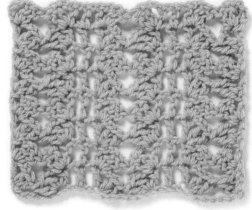

Multiple of 10 + 12

INSTRUCTIONS
SQUARE
Row 1 (RS): 2 dc in 6th ch from hook (*first 5 chs count as first dc and ch-2 sp*), *sk next 5 chs, (2 dc, ch 2, dc) in next ch, ch 1, sk next ch, dc in next ch, ch 1, sk next ch, (dc, ch 2, 2 dc) in next ch, rep from * across to last 6 chs, ch 5, sk next 5 chs, (2 dc, ch 2, dc) in last ch, turn.

Row 2: Ch 5 (*counts as first dc and ch-2 sp*), 2 dc in same st, *sk next 4 dc**, (2 dc, ch 2, dc) in next dc, ch 1, dc in next dc, ch 1, (dc, ch 2, 2 dc) in next dc, rep from * across, ending last rep at **, (2 dc, ch 2, dc) in 5th ch of beg 5 sk chs, turn.

Row 3: Ch 5 (*counts as first dc and ch-2 sp*), 2 dc in same st, *sk next 4 dc**, (2 dc, ch 2, dc) in next dc, ch 1, dc in next dc, ch 1, (dc, ch 2, 2 dc) in next dc, rep from * across, ending last rep at **, (2 dc, ch 2, dc) in 3rd ch of beg ch-5, turn.

Rep row 3 for pattern. ∎

Square 47

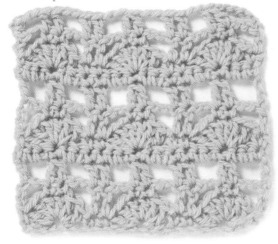

Multiple of 7 + 8

PATTERN NOTE
Chain-5 at beginning of row counts as first double crochet and chain-2 space unless otherwise stated.

INSTRUCTIONS
SQUARE
Row 1 (RS): Sc in 2nd ch from hook, sk next 2 chs, 6 dc in next ch, sk next 2 chs, sc in next ch, [sc in next ch, sk next 2 chs, 6 dc in next ch, sk next 2 chs, sc in next ch] across, turn.

Row 2: Ch 5 (*see Pattern Note*), sk first 3 sts, *sc in 3rd and 4th dc of next 6-dc group, ch 2**, dc in each of next 2 sc, ch 2, rep from * across, ending last rep at **, dc in last st, turn.

Row 3: Ch 5, dc dec in next 2 sc, ch 2, [dc in each of next 2 sts, ch 2, dc dec in next 2 sts, ch 2] across to last st, dc in 3rd ch of beg ch-5, turn.

Row 4: Ch 1, sc in first st, 2 sc in each ch-2 sp and sc in each st across to last st, sc in 3rd ch of beg ch-5, turn.

Row 5: Ch 1, sc in first st, sk next 2 sts, 6 dc in next st, sk next 2 sts, sc in next st, [sc in next st, sk next 2 sts, 6 dc in next st, sk next 2 sts, sc in next st] across, turn.

Rep rows 2–5 for pattern. ∎

Square 48

Multiple of 5 + 10

SPECIAL STITCH
Picot: Ch 3, sl st in 3rd ch from hook.

INSTRUCTIONS
SQUARE
Row 1 (RS): Sc in 8th ch from hook (*first 7 chs count as dc, ch-3 sp and sk ch*), **picot** (*see Special Stitch*), [ch 3, sk next ch, dc in each of next 2 chs, ch 3, sk next ch, sc in next ch, picot] across to last 2 chs, ch 3, sk next ch, dc in last ch, turn

Row 2: Ch 3 (*counts as first dc*), sk first st, dc in next ch-3 sp, [ch 1, dc in first ch-3 sp after next picot, dc in each of next 2 sts, dc in next ch-3 sp] across to last picot, ch 1, dc in last ch-3 sp, dc in 4th ch of beg 7 sk chs, turn.

Row 3: Ch 6 (*counts as first dc and ch-3 sp*), sk first 2 sts, [sc in next ch-1 sp, picot, ch 3, sk next st, dc in each of next 2 sts, ch 3, sk next st] across to last ch-1 sp, sc in last ch-1 sp, picot, ch 3, sk next st, dc in 3rd ch of beg ch-3, turn.

Row 4: Ch 3, sk first st, dc in next ch-3 sp, [ch 1, dc in first ch-3 sp after next picot, dc in each of next 2 sts, dc in next ch-3 sp] across to last picot, ch 1, dc in last ch-3 sp, dc 3rd ch of beg ch-6, turn.

Rep rows 3 and 4 for pattern, ending last rep with row 3. ∎

Square 49

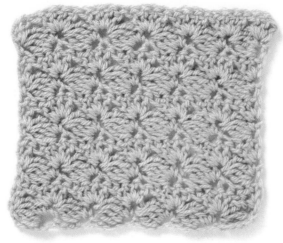

Multiple of 4 + 2

SPECIAL STITCH
Cluster (cl): Yo, insert hook in indicated place, yo, pull lp through, yo, pull through 2 lps on hook, [yo, insert hook in same place, yo, pull lp through, yo, pull through 2 lps on hook] twice, yo, pull through all 4 lps on hook.

INSTRUCTIONS
SQUARE
Row 1 (RS): (Sc, ch 3, **cl**—*see Special Stitch*) in 2nd ch from hook, [sk next 3 chs, (sc, ch 3, cl) in next ch] across, turn.

Row 2: Ch 3 *(counts as first dc)*, dc in same st, 4 dc in each sc across with 3 dc in last st, turn.

Row 3: Ch 1, (sc, ch 3, cl) in first st, (sc, ch 3, cl) in 2nd dc of each 4-dc group across, sc in 3rd ch of beg ch-3, turn.

Rep rows 2 and 3 for pattern. ∎

Square 50

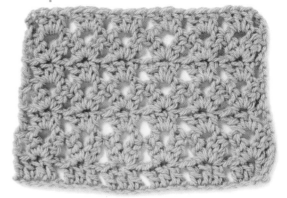

Multiple of 4 + 7

PATTERN NOTE
Chain-3 at beginning of row counts as first double crochet unless otherwise stated.

SPECIAL STITCHES
Cluster (cl): Yo, insert hook in indicated place, yo, pull lp through, yo, pull through 2 lps on hook, yo, insert hook in same place, yo, pull lp through, yo, pull lp through 2 lps on hook, yo, pull through all 3 lps on hook.

Shell: (**Cl**—*see Special Stitches*, ch 3, cl) in indicated place.

INSTRUCTIONS
SQUARE
Row 1 (RS): Dc in 4th ch from hook *(first 3 chs count as first dc)*, dc in each of next 2 chs, [ch 1, sk next ch, dc in each of next 3 chs] across to last ch, dc in last ch, turn.

Row 2: **Ch 3** *(see Pattern Note)*, sk first dc, **shell** *(see Special Stitches)* in center st of each 3-dc group across to last st, dc in 3rd ch of beg sk 3 chs, turn.

Row 3: Ch 3, 3 dc in ch sp of each shell across to last st, dc in 3rd ch of beg ch-3, turn.

Row 4: Ch 3, sk first dc, shell in center st of each 3-dc group across to last st, dc in 3rd ch of beg ch-3, turn.

Rep rows 3 and 4 for pattern, ending last rep with row 3. ∎

STITCH GUIDE

STITCH ABBREVIATIONS

beg	begin/begins/beginning
bpdc	back post double crochet
bpsc	back post single crochet
bptr	back post treble crochet
CC	contrasting color
ch(s)	chain(s)
ch-	refers to chain or space previously made (i.e., ch-1 space)
ch sp(s)	chain space(s)
cl(s)	cluster(s)
cm	centimeter(s)
dc	double crochet (singular/plural)
dc dec	double crochet 2 or more stitches together, as indicated
dec	decrease/decreases/decreasing
dtr	double treble crochet
ext	extended
fpdc	front post double crochet
fpsc	front post single crochet
fptr	front post treble crochet
g	gram(s)
hdc	half double crochet
hdc dec	half double crochet 2 or more stitches together, as indicated
inc	increase/increases/increasing
lp(s)	loop(s)
MC	main color
mm	millimeter(s)
oz	ounce(s)
pc	popcorn(s)
rem	remain/remains/remaining
rep(s)	repeat(s)
rnd(s)	round(s)
RS	right side
sc	single crochet (singular/plural)
sc dec	single crochet 2 or more stitches together, as indicated
sk	skip/skipped/skipping
sl st(s)	slip stitch(es)
sp(s)	space(s)/spaced
st(s)	stitch(es)
tog	together
tr	treble crochet
trtr	triple treble
WS	wrong side
yd(s)	yard(s)
yo	yarn over

YARN CONVERSION

OUNCES TO GRAMS		GRAMS TO OUNCES	
1	28.4	25	7/8
2	56.7	40	1 2/3
3	85.0	50	1 3/4
4	113.4	100	3 1/2

UNITED STATES		UNITED KINGDOM
sl st (slip stitch)	=	sc (single crochet)
sc (single crochet)	=	dc (double crochet)
hdc (half double crochet)	=	htr (half treble crochet)
dc (double crochet)	=	tr (treble crochet)
tr (treble crochet)	=	dtr (double treble crochet)
dtr (double treble crochet)	=	ttr (triple treble crochet)
skip	=	miss

Single crochet decrease (sc dec): (Insert hook, yo, draw lp through) in each of the sts indicated, yo, draw through all lps on hook.

Example of 2-sc dec

Half double crochet decrease (hdc dec): (Yo, insert hook, yo, draw lp through) in each of the sts indicated, yo, draw through all lps on hook.

Example of 2-hdc dec

Reverse single crochet (reverse sc): Ch 1, sk first st, working from left to right, insert hook in next st from front to back, draw up lp on hook, yo and draw through both lps on hook.

Chain (ch): Yo, pull through lp on hook.

Single crochet (sc): Insert hook in st, yo, pull through st, yo, pull through both lps on hook.

Double crochet (dc): Yo, insert hook in st, yo, pull through st, [yo, pull through 2 lps] twice.

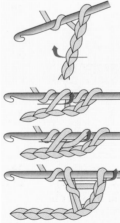

Double crochet decrease (dc dec): (Yo, insert hook, yo, draw lp through, yo, draw through 2 lps on hook) in each of the sts indicated, yo, draw through all lps on hook.

Example of 2-dc dec

Front loop (front lp) Back loop (back lp)

Front Loop   Back Loop

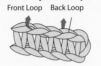

Front post stitch (fp): Back post stitch (bp): When working post st, insert hook from right to left around post of st on previous row.

Back   Front

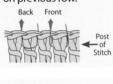

Post of Stitch

Half double crochet (hdc): Yo, insert hook in st, yo, pull through st, yo, pull through all 3 lps on hook.

Double treble crochet (dtr): Yo 3 times, insert hook in st, yo, pull through st, [yo, pull through 2 lps] 4 times.

Treble crochet decrease (tr dec): Holding back last lp of each st, tr in each of the sts indicated, yo, pull through all lps on hook.

Example of 2-tr dec

Slip stitch (sl st): Insert hook in st, pull through both lps on hook.

Chain color change (ch color change) Yo with new color, draw through last lp on hook.

Double crochet color change (dc color change) Drop first color, yo with new color, draw through last 2 lps of st.

Treble crochet (tr): Yo twice, insert hook in st, yo, pull through st, [yo, pull through 2 lps] 3 times.

Metric Conversion Charts

METRIC CONVERSIONS

yards	x	.9144	=	metres (m)
yards	x	91.44	=	centimetres (cm)
inches	x	2.54	=	centimetres (cm)
inches	x	25.40	=	millimetres (mm)
inches	x	.0254	=	metres (m)

centimetres	x	.3937	=	inches
metres	x	1.0936	=	yards

INCHES INTO MILLIMETRES & CENTIMETRES (Rounded off slightly)

inches	mm	cm	inches	cm	inches	cm	inches	cm
1/8	3	0.3	5	12.5	21	53.5	38	96.5
1/4	6	0.6	5 1/2	14	22	56	39	99
3/8	10	1	6	15	23	58.5	40	101.5
1/2	13	1.3	7	18	24	61	41	104
5/8	15	1.5	8	20.5	25	63.5	42	106.5
3/4	20	2	9	23	26	66	43	109
7/8	22	2.2	10	25.5	27	68.5	44	112
1	25	2.5	11	28	28	71	45	114.5
1 1/4	32	3.2	12	30.5	29	73.5	46	117
1 1/2	38	3.8	13	33	30	76	47	119.5
1 3/4	45	4.5	14	35.5	31	79	48	122
2	50	5	15	38	32	81.5	49	124.5
2 1/2	65	6.5	16	40.5	33	84	50	127
3	75	7.5	17	43	34	86.5		
3 1/2	90	9	18	46	35	89		
4	100	10	19	48.5	36	91.5		
4 1/2	115	11.5	20	51	37	94		

KNITTING NEEDLES CONVERSION CHART

Canada/U.S.	0	1	2	3	4	5	6	7	8	9	10	10½	11	13	15
Metric (mm)	2	2¼	2¾	3¼	3½	3¾	4	4½	5	5½	6	6½	8	9	10

CROCHET HOOKS CONVERSION CHART

Canada/U.S.	1/B	2/C	3/D	4/E	5/F	6/G	8/H	9/I	10/J	10½/K	N
Metric (mm)	2.25	2.75	3.25	3.5	3.75	4.25	5	5.5	6	6.5	9.0

ISBN: 978-1-59635-302-2

456789